My Own Book of
Numbers

ISBN 13: 978-1-964243-58-0
ISBN 10: 1-964243-58-0

Permission request(s) should be submitted to the publisher in writing at one of the addresses below:
CHEETAH® Toys & More, LLC
207 Main Street, 3rd Floor
Hartford, CT 06106 USA

Port Antonio PO
Portland, Jamaica

info@mycheetahinc.com
paulettetrowers@yahoo.com
WhatsApp: 860-781-1726
876-909-6311

My Own Book of
Numbers

My Own Book of
Numbers

1   2   3   4   5   6   7   8   9   10

My Own Book of
Numbers

1 2 3 4 5 6 7 8 9 10

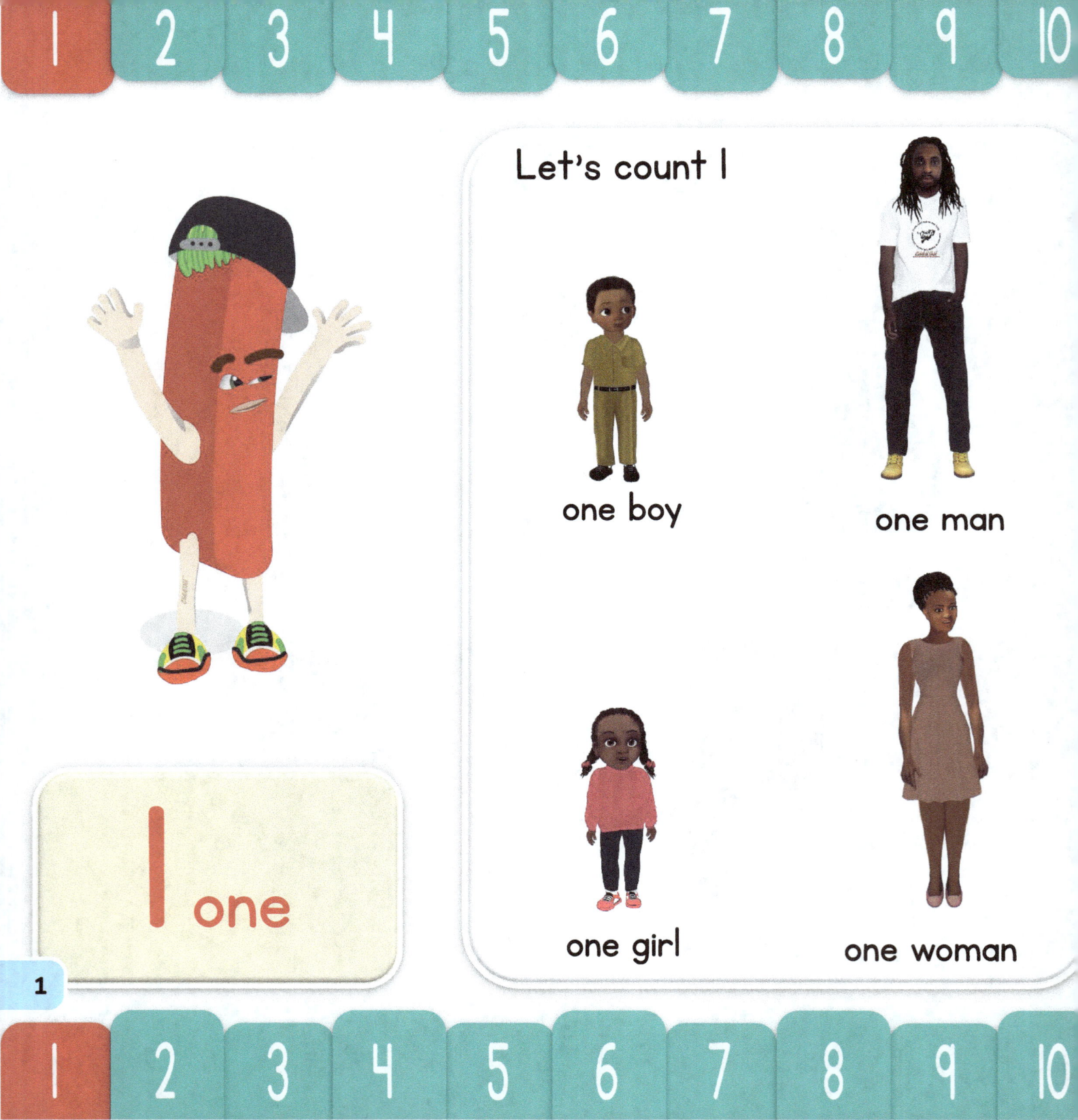

1 one

Let's count 1

one boy

one man

one girl

one woman

Trace number!

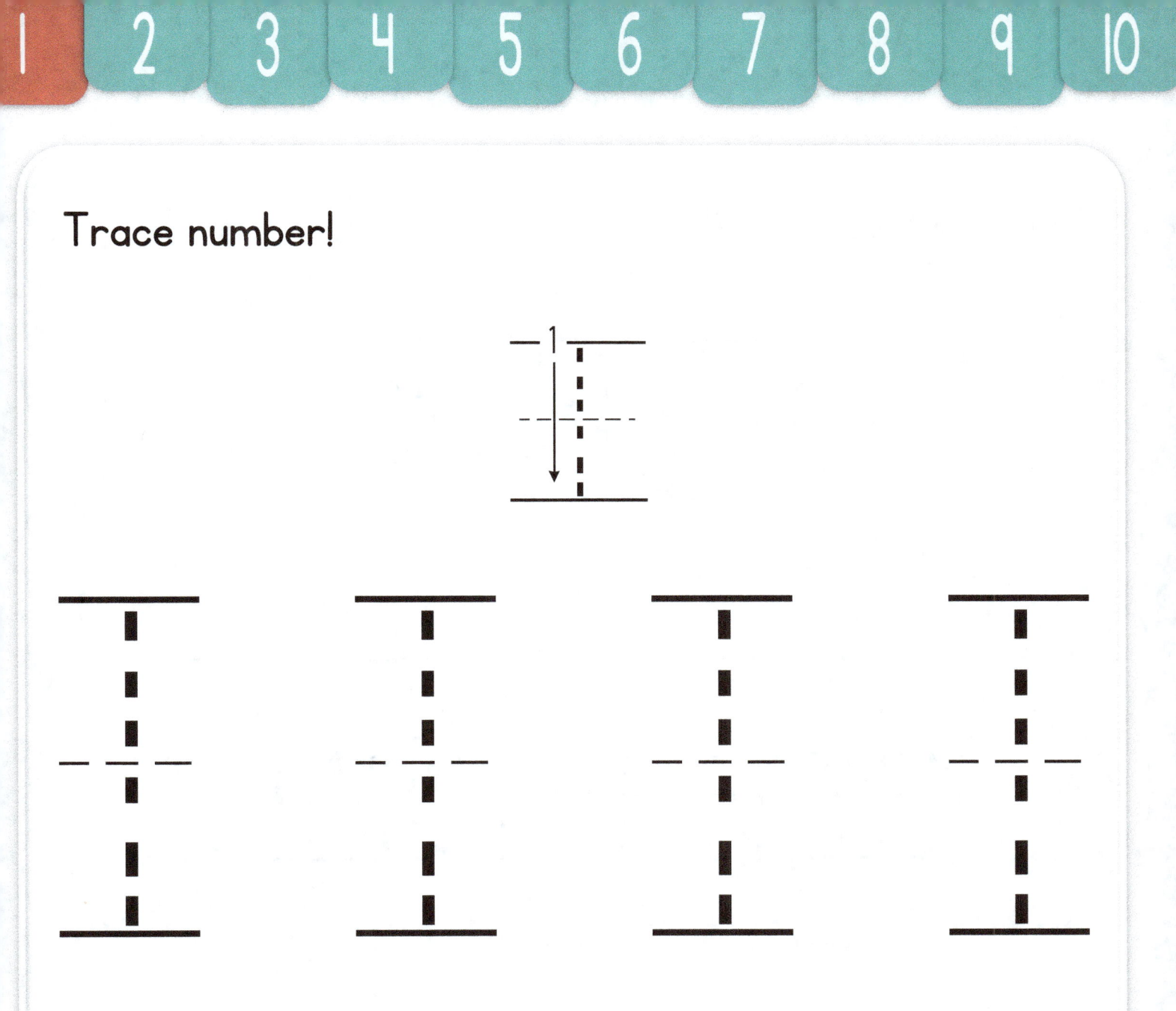

Trace number name!

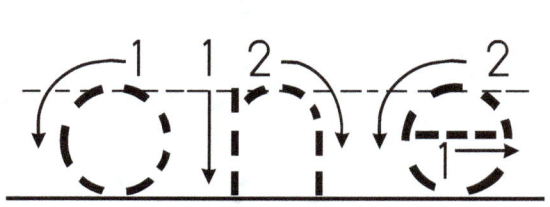

Put Counter on the frame

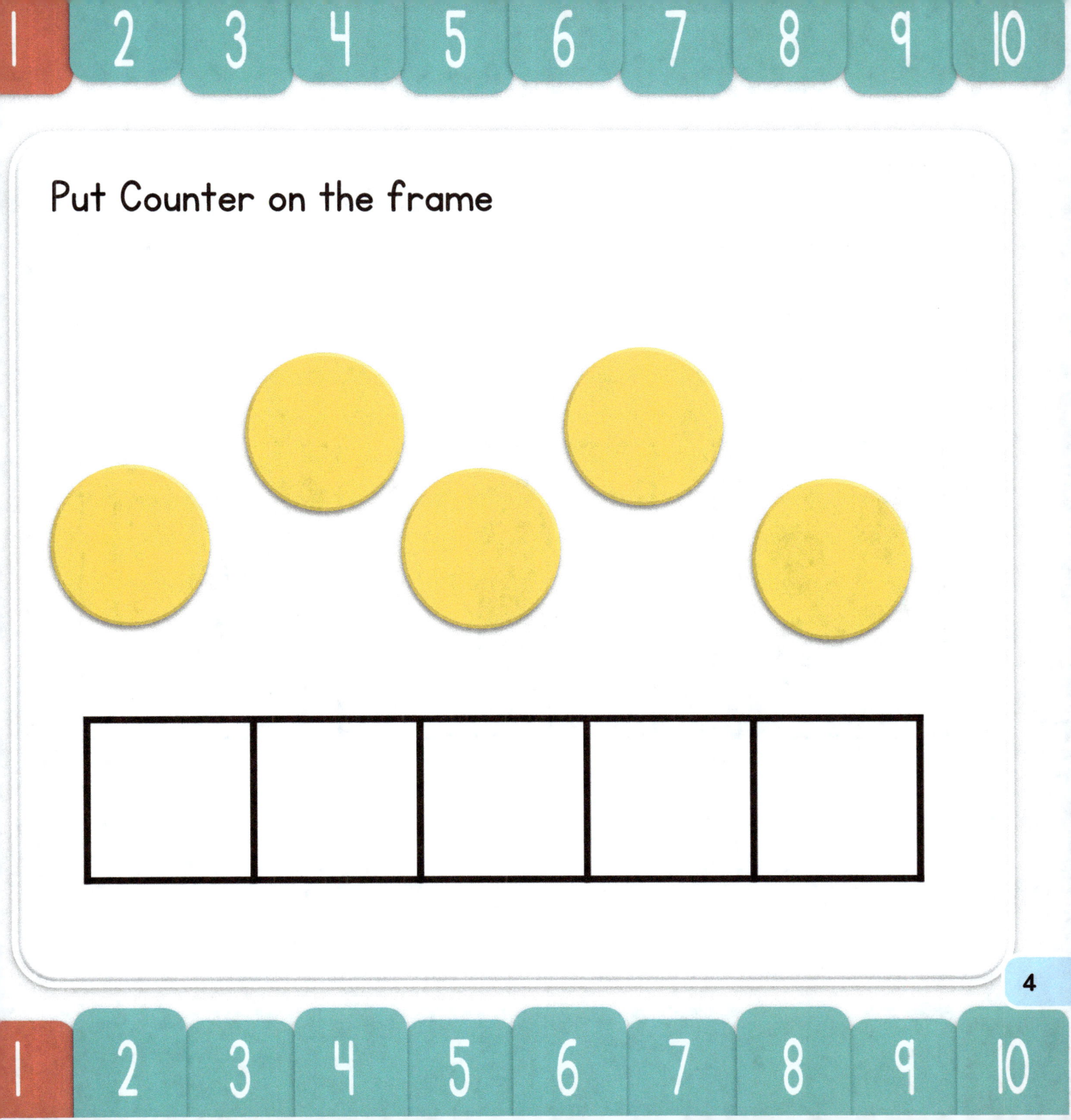

Activity 1

Choose the box with 1 person.

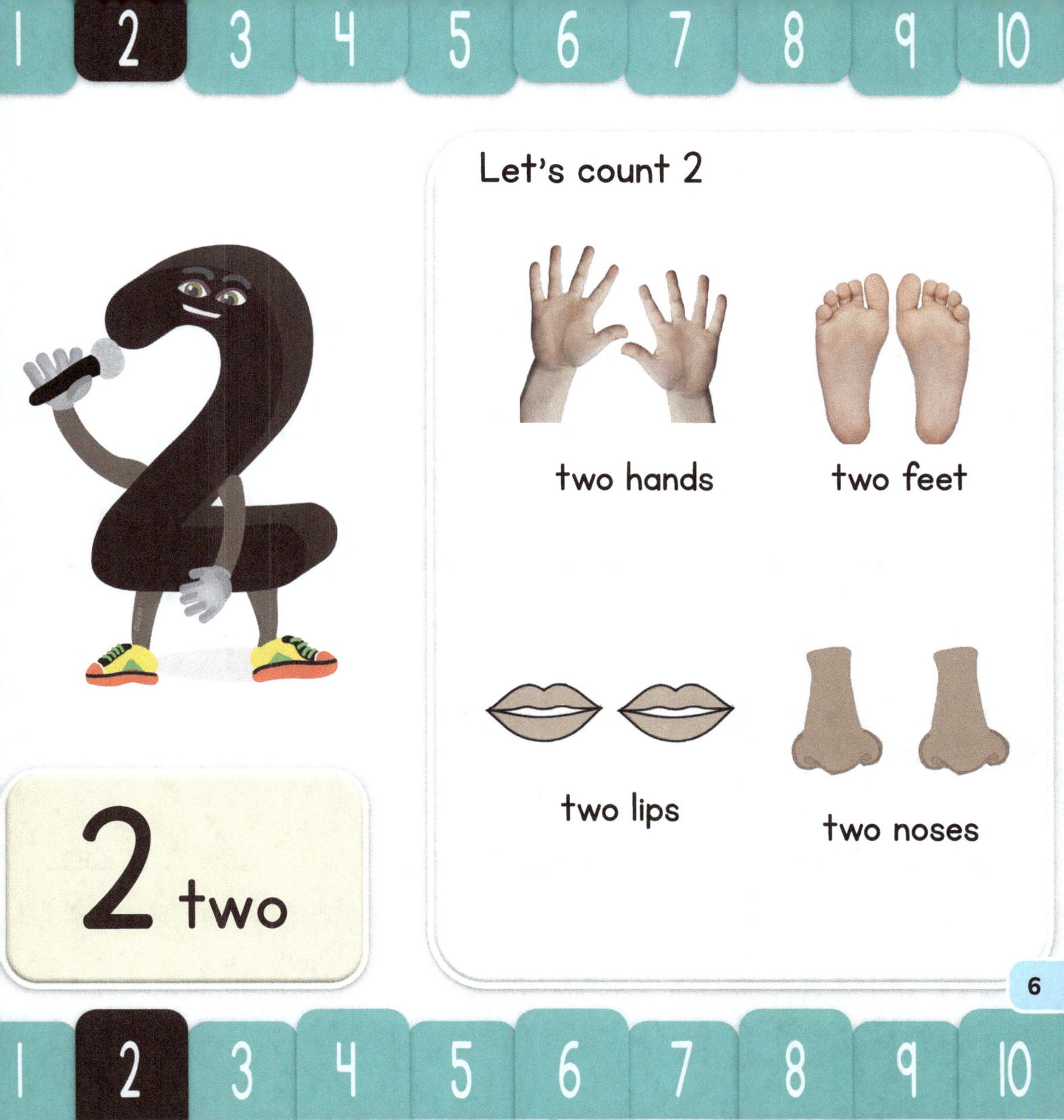

2 two

Let's count 2

two hands

two feet

two lips

two noses

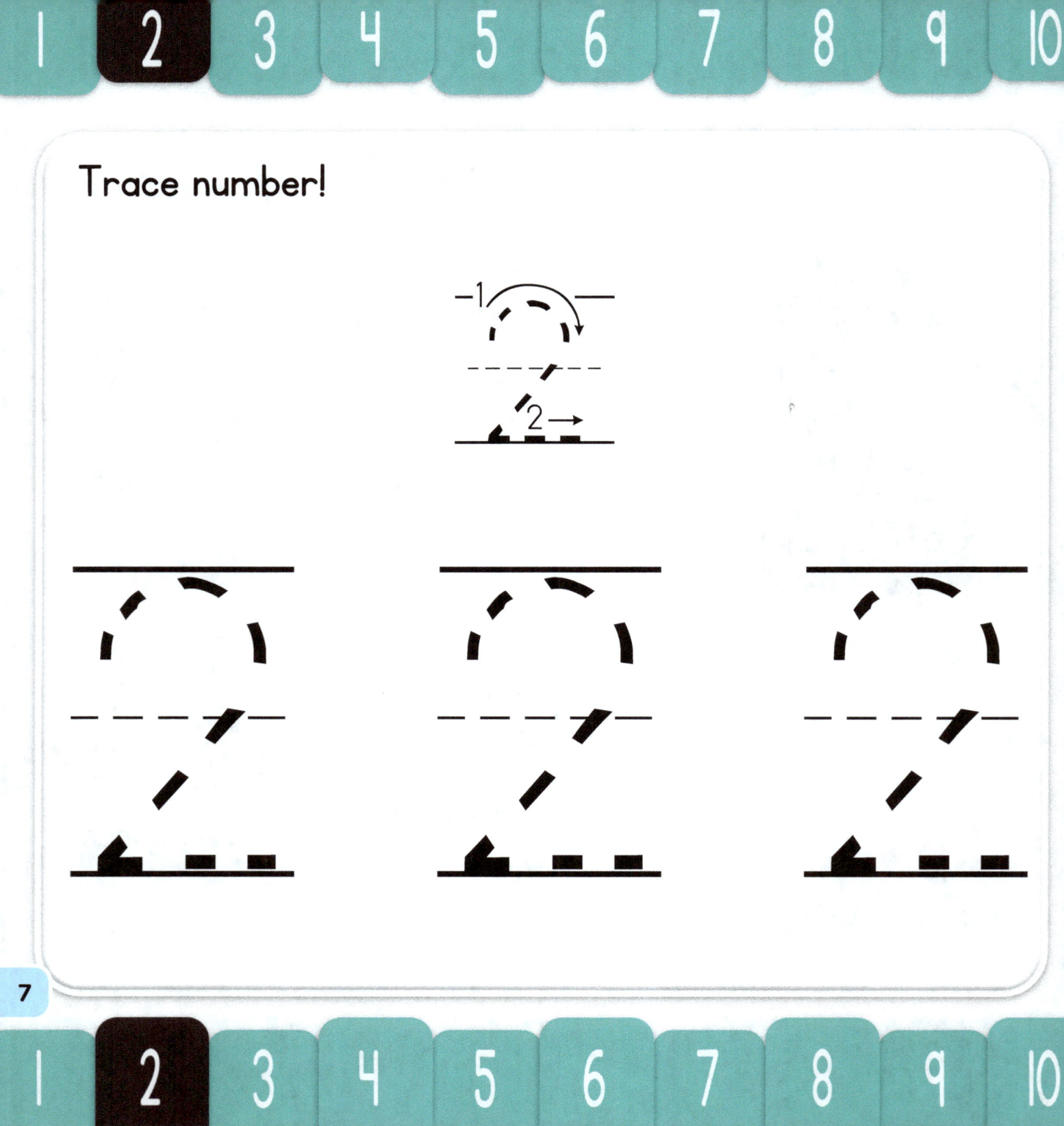

Trace number!

Trace number name!

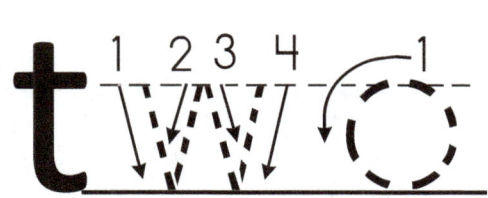

Put Counter on the frame

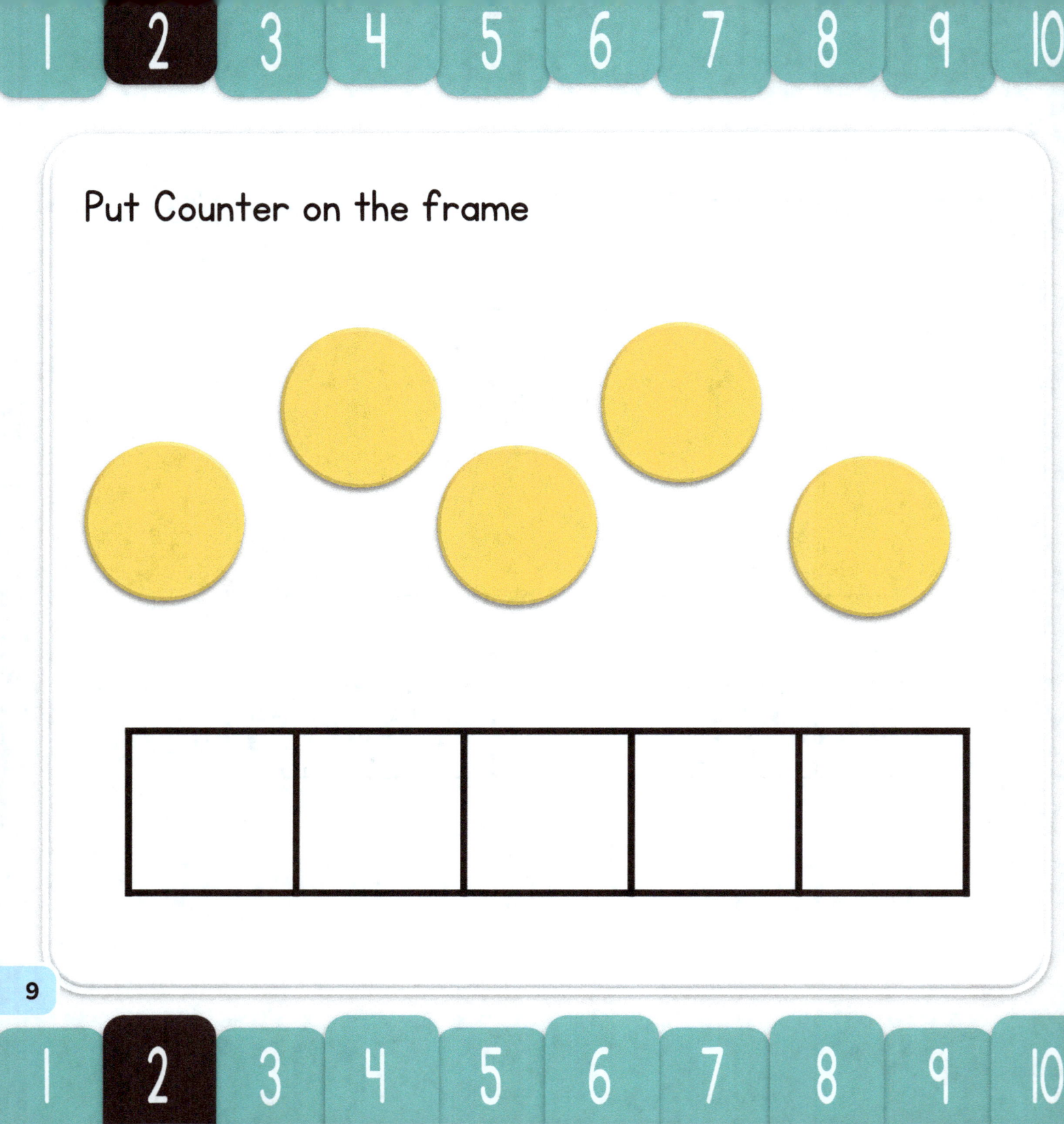

Activity 2

Colour the group with 2 body parts.

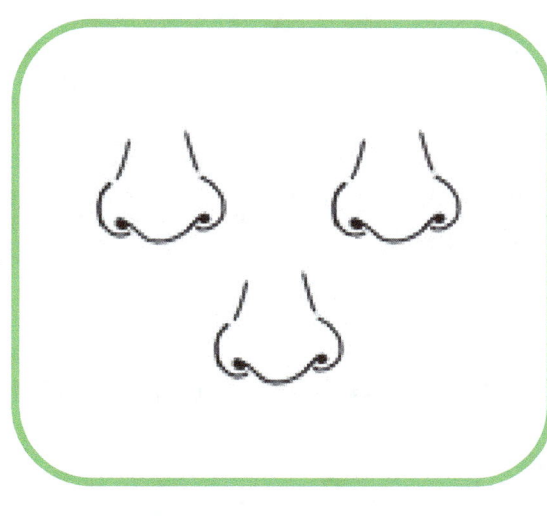

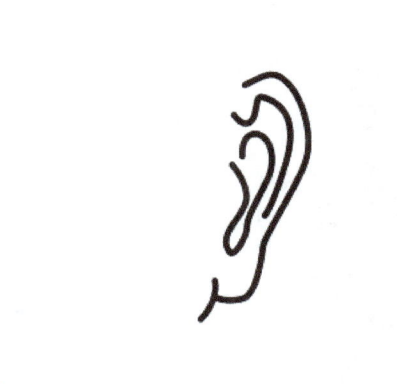

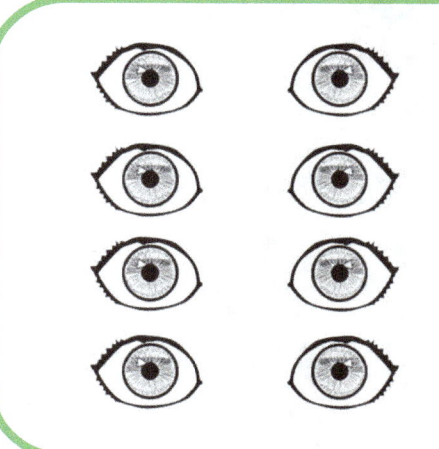

3 three

11

Let's count 3

three candles

three cakes

three hats

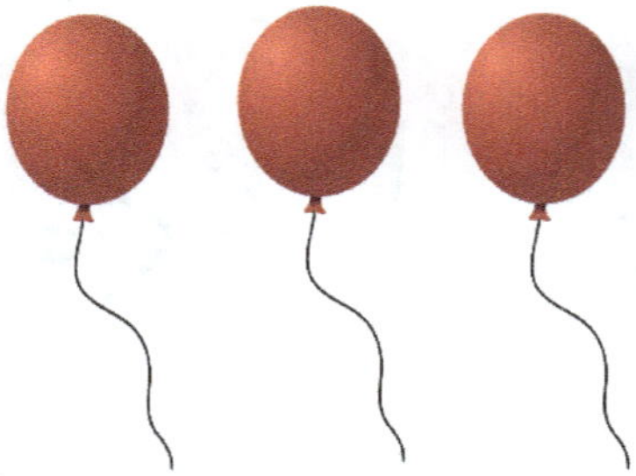

three balloons

Trace number!

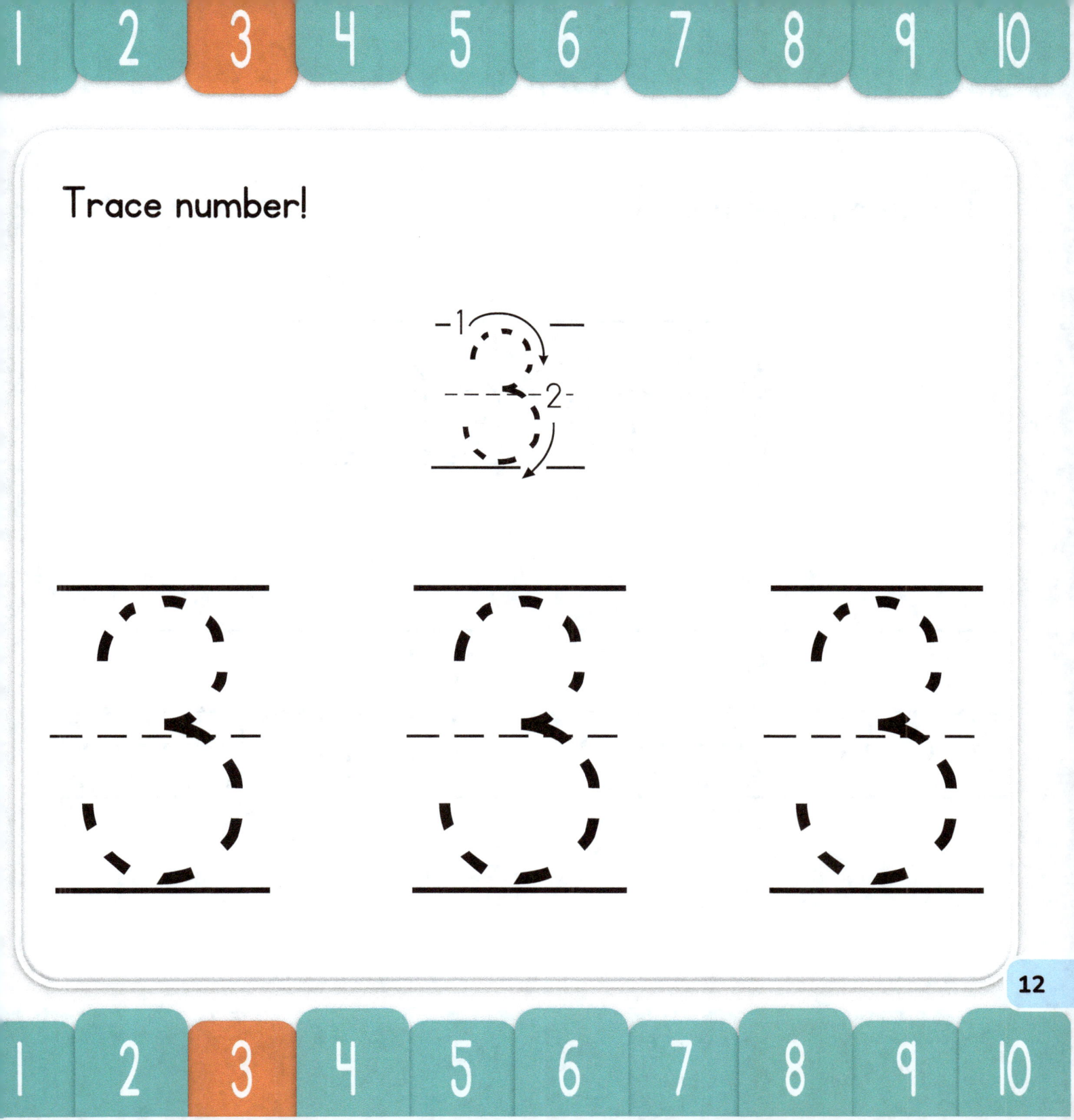

Trace number name!

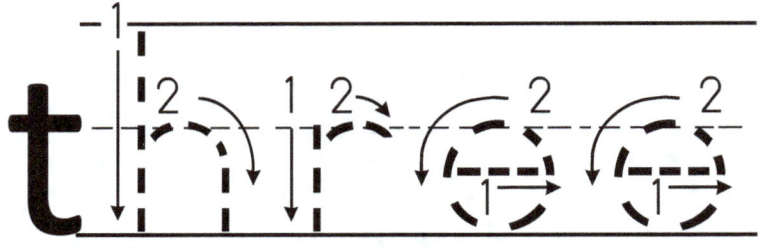

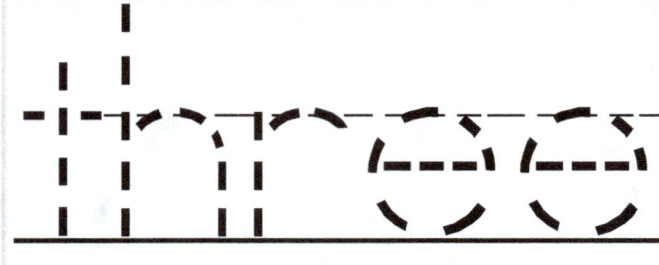   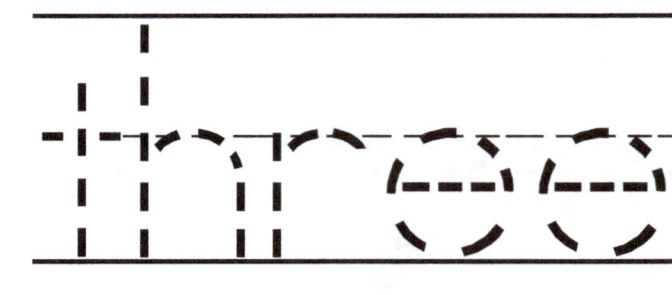

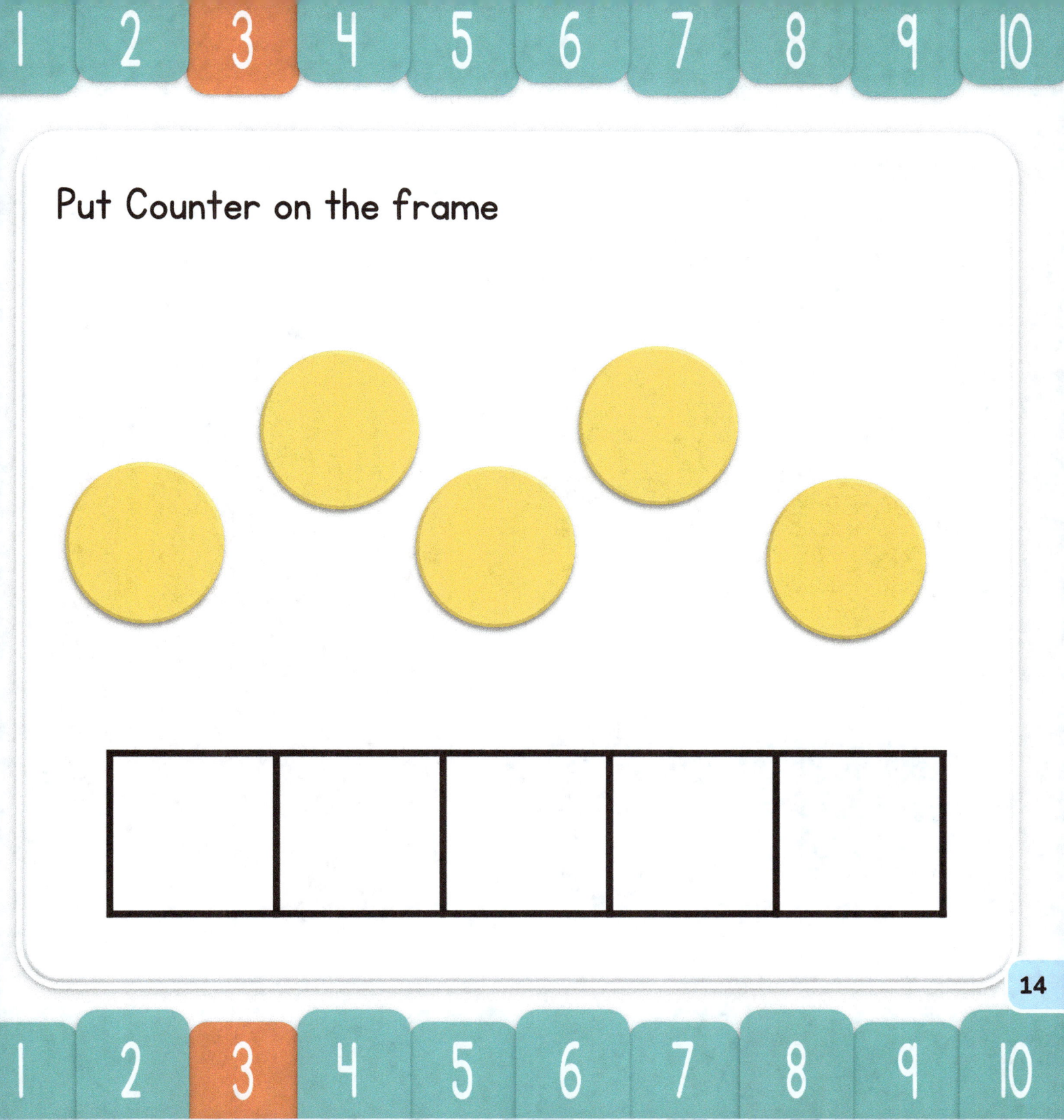

Put Counter on the frame

Activity 3

Put three birthday gifts in the bag.

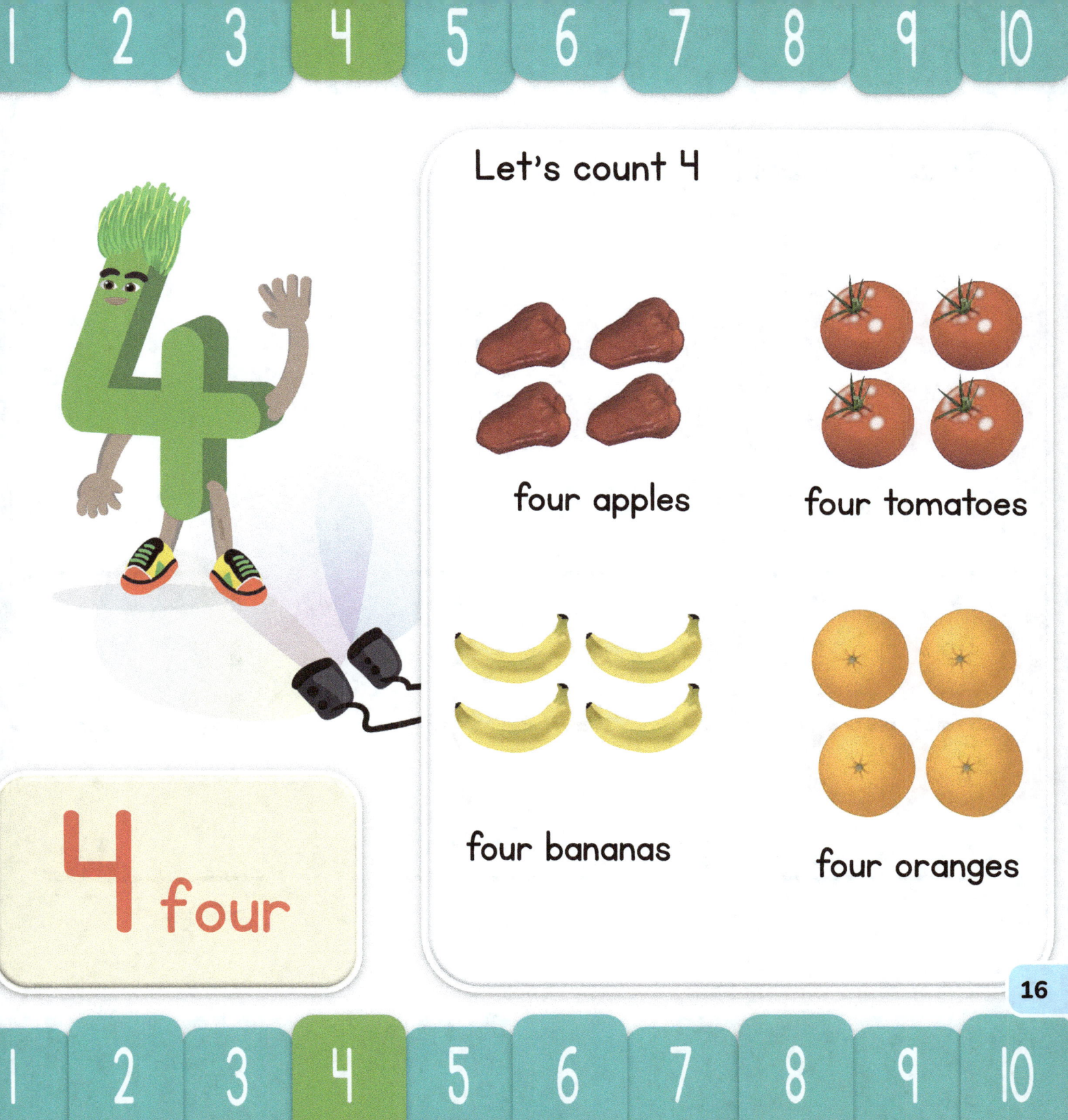

Let's count 4

four apples

four tomatoes

four bananas

four oranges

4 four

Trace number!

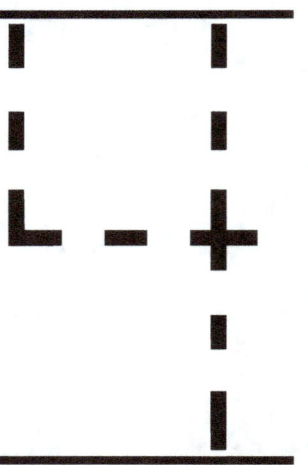

Trace number name!

four

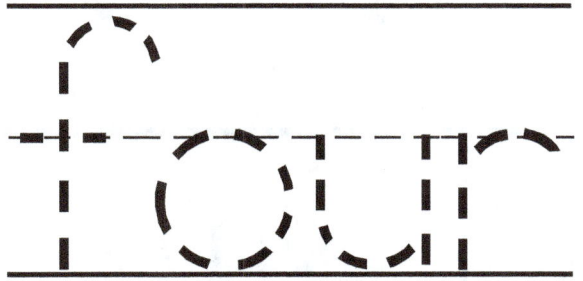 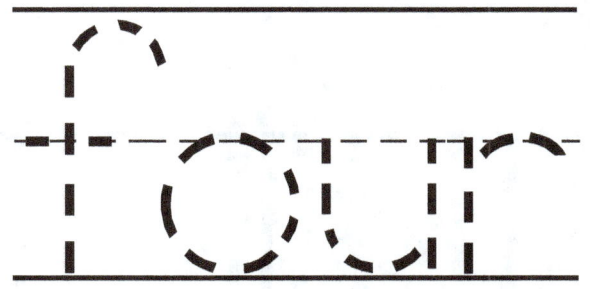

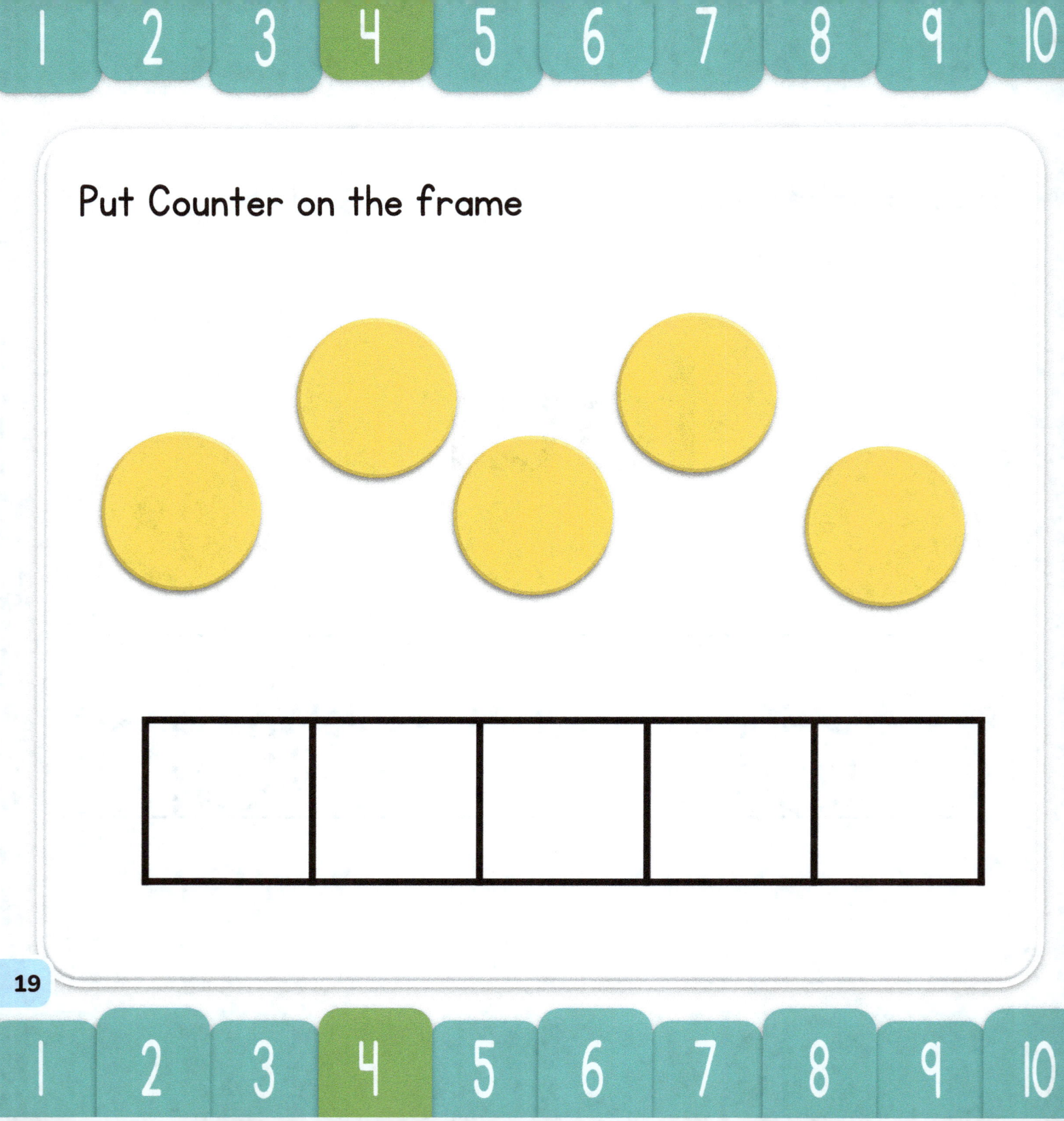

Put Counter on the frame

Activity 4

Choose the set with 4 objects

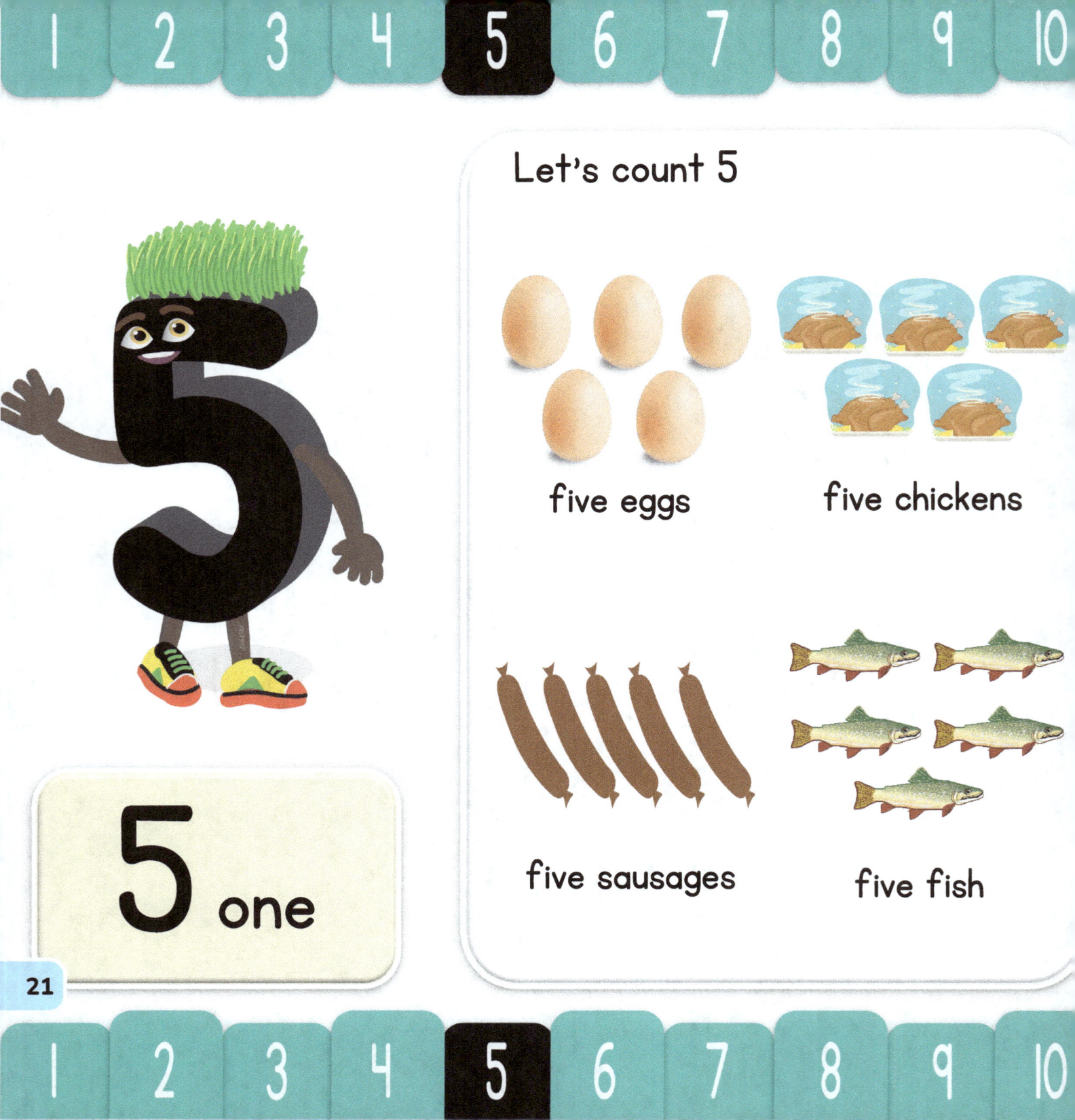

Let's count 5

five eggs

five chickens

five sausages

five fish

5 one

Trace number!

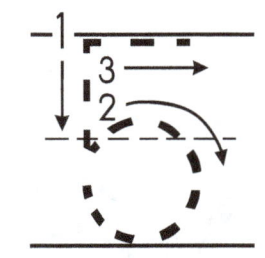

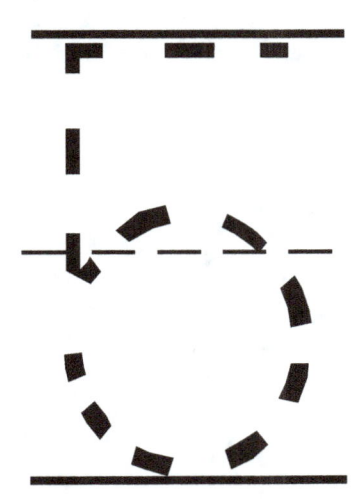 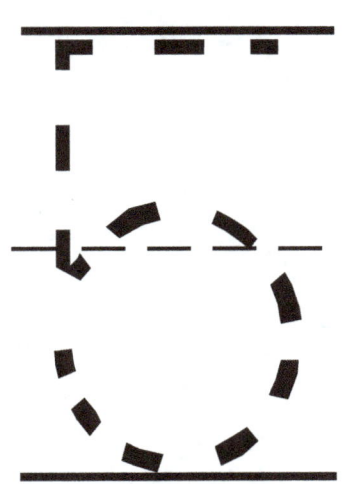 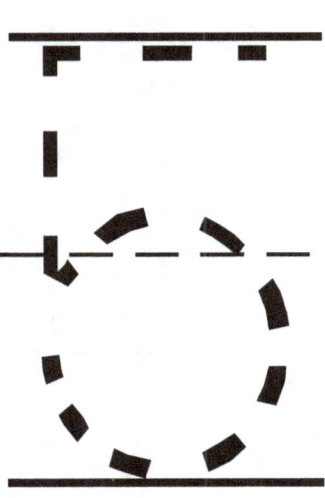

Trace number name!

five

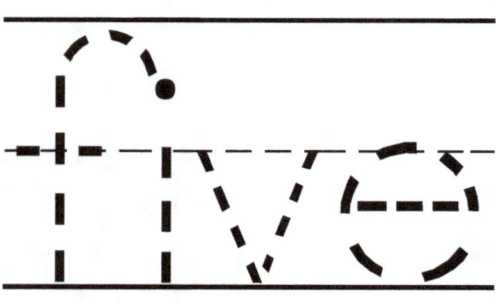 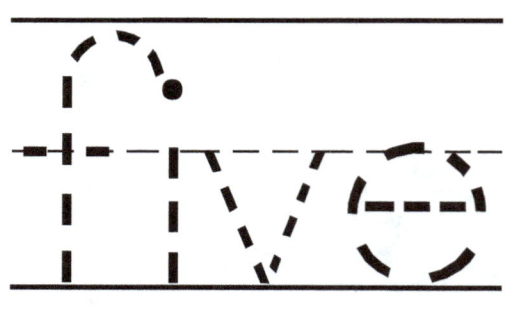

Put Counter on the frame

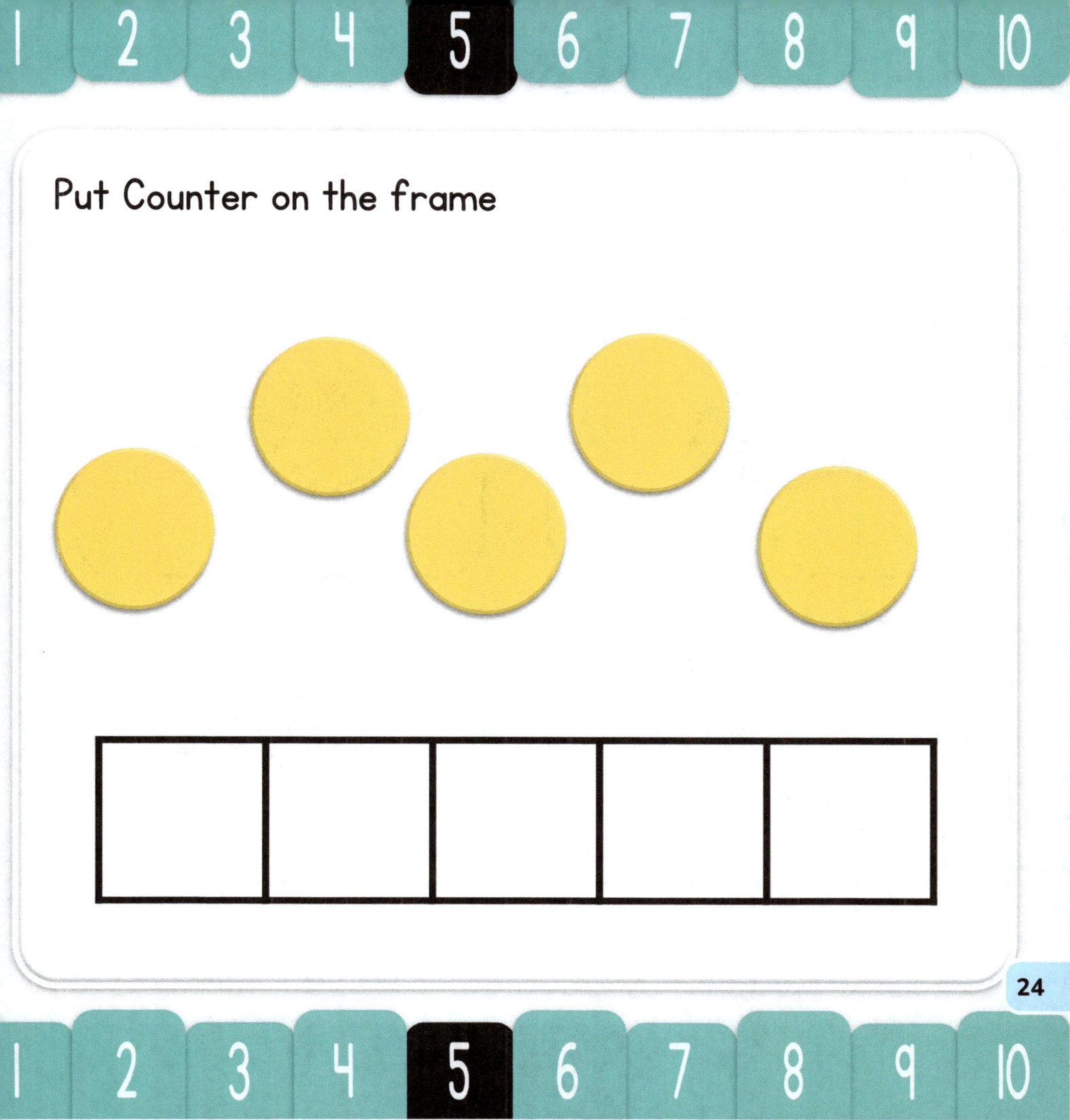

Activity 5

Choose the group with 5 objects.

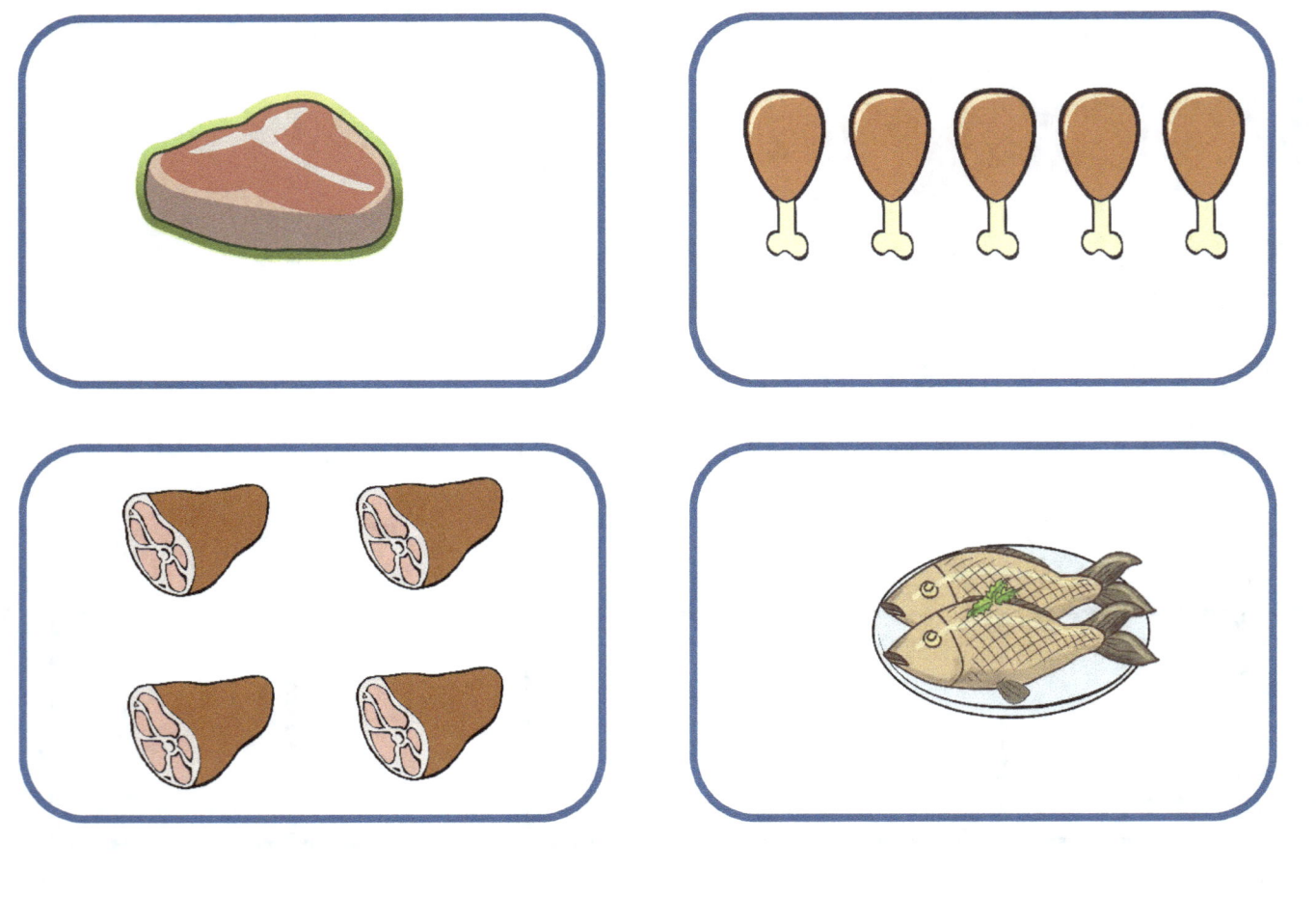

Let's count 6

six fish

six puppies

six birds

six kittens

6 six

Trace number!

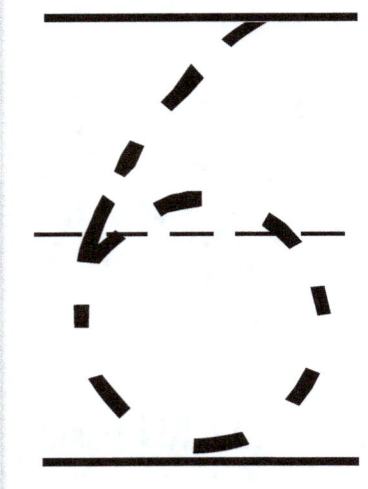
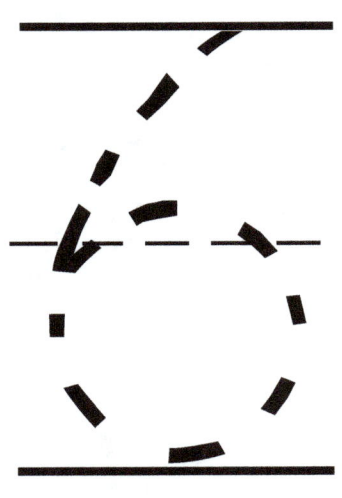
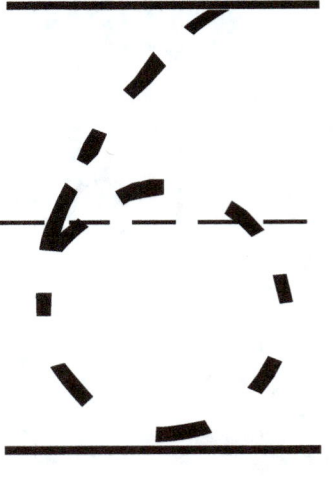

Trace number name!

six

28

Put Counter on the frame

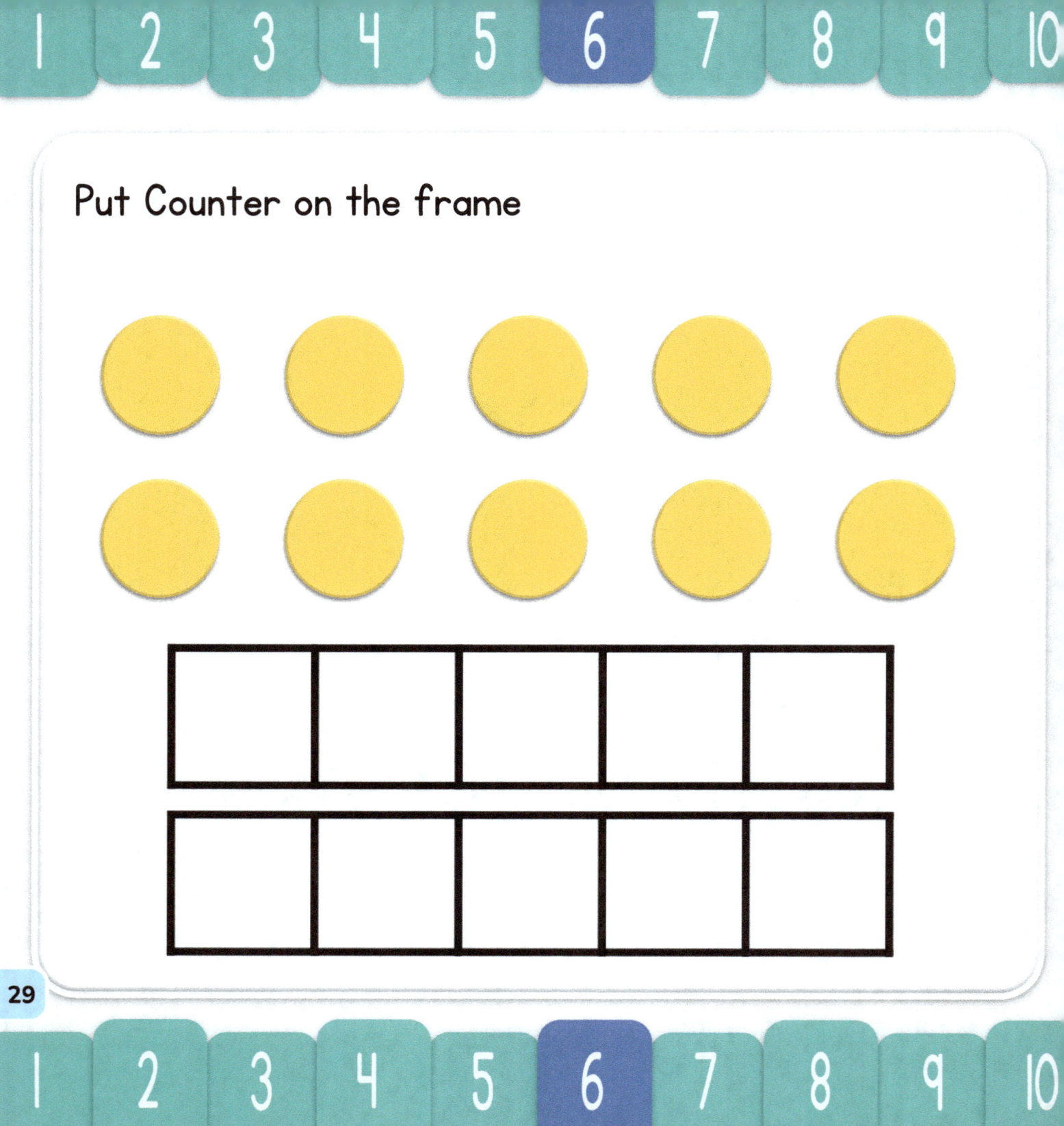

Activity 6

Colour the group with 6 pets.

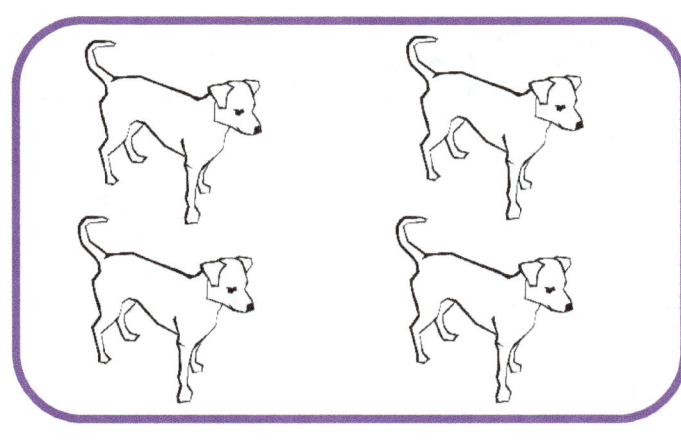

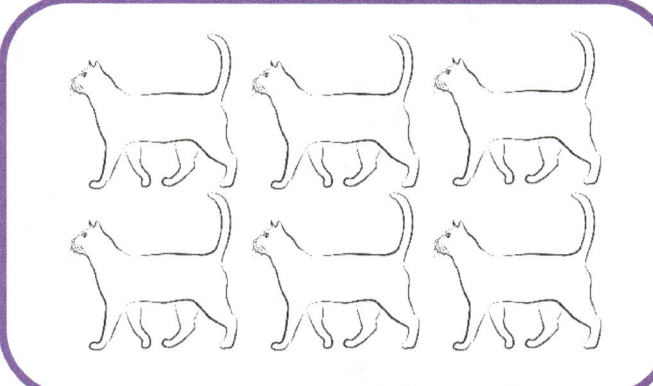

Let's count 7

seven cows

seven roosters

seven rabbit

seven goats

7 seven

31

Trace number!

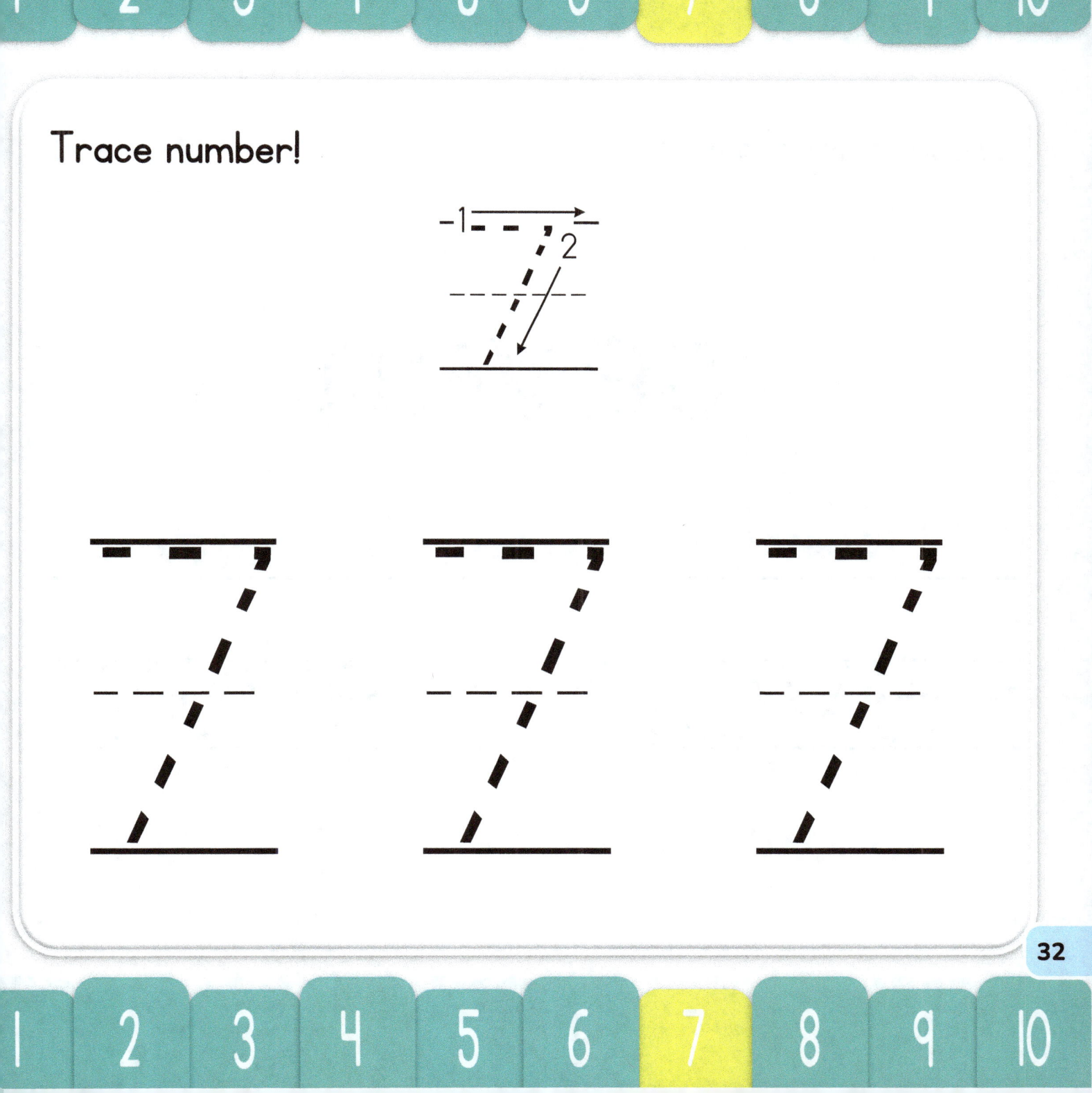

Trace number name!

seven

 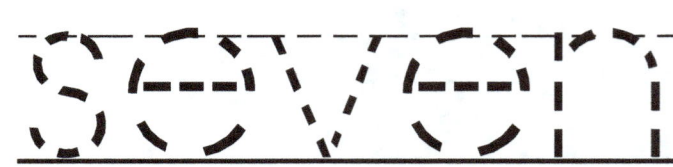

Put Counter on the frame

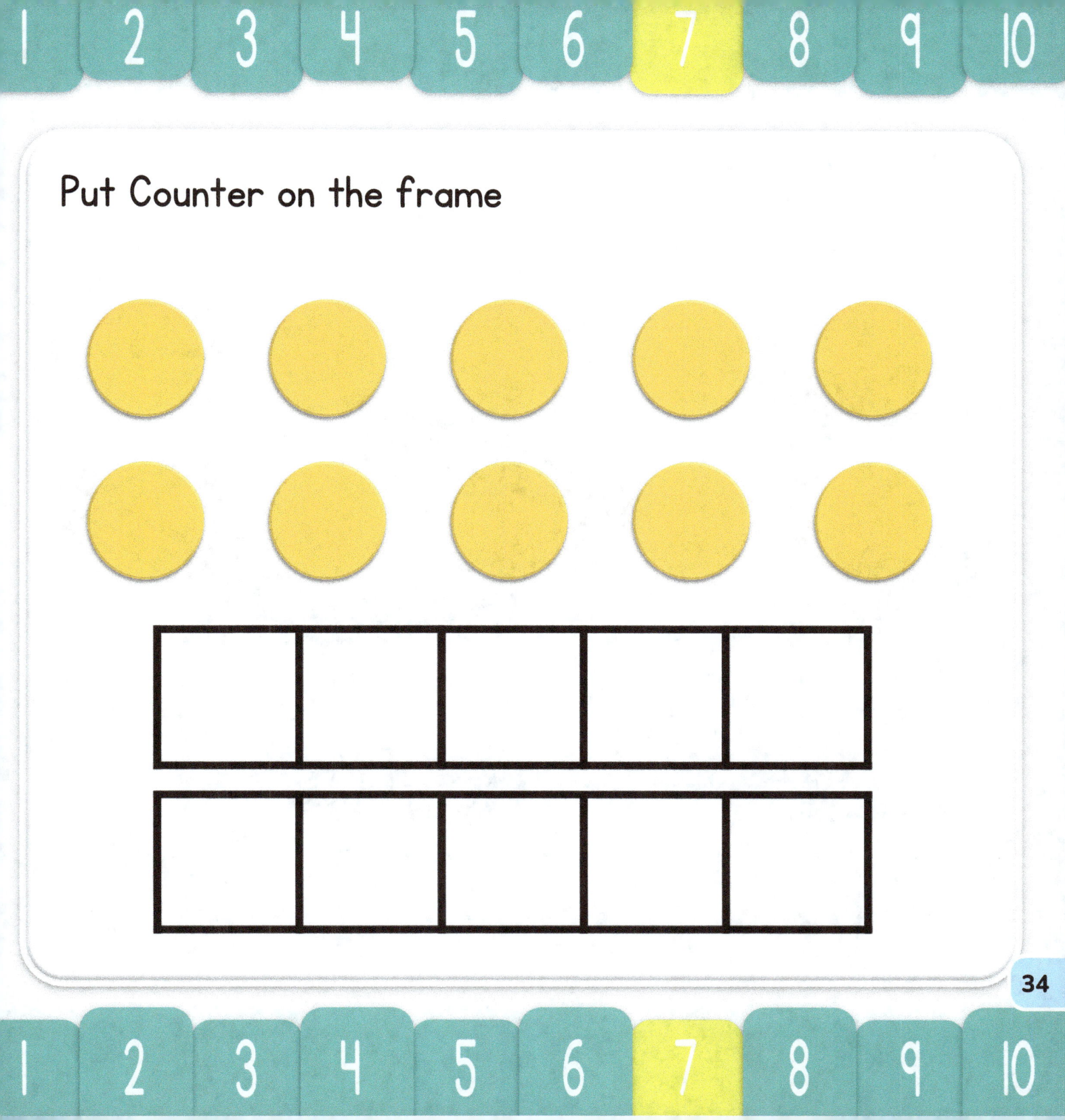

Activity 7

Put 7 animals in the pen.

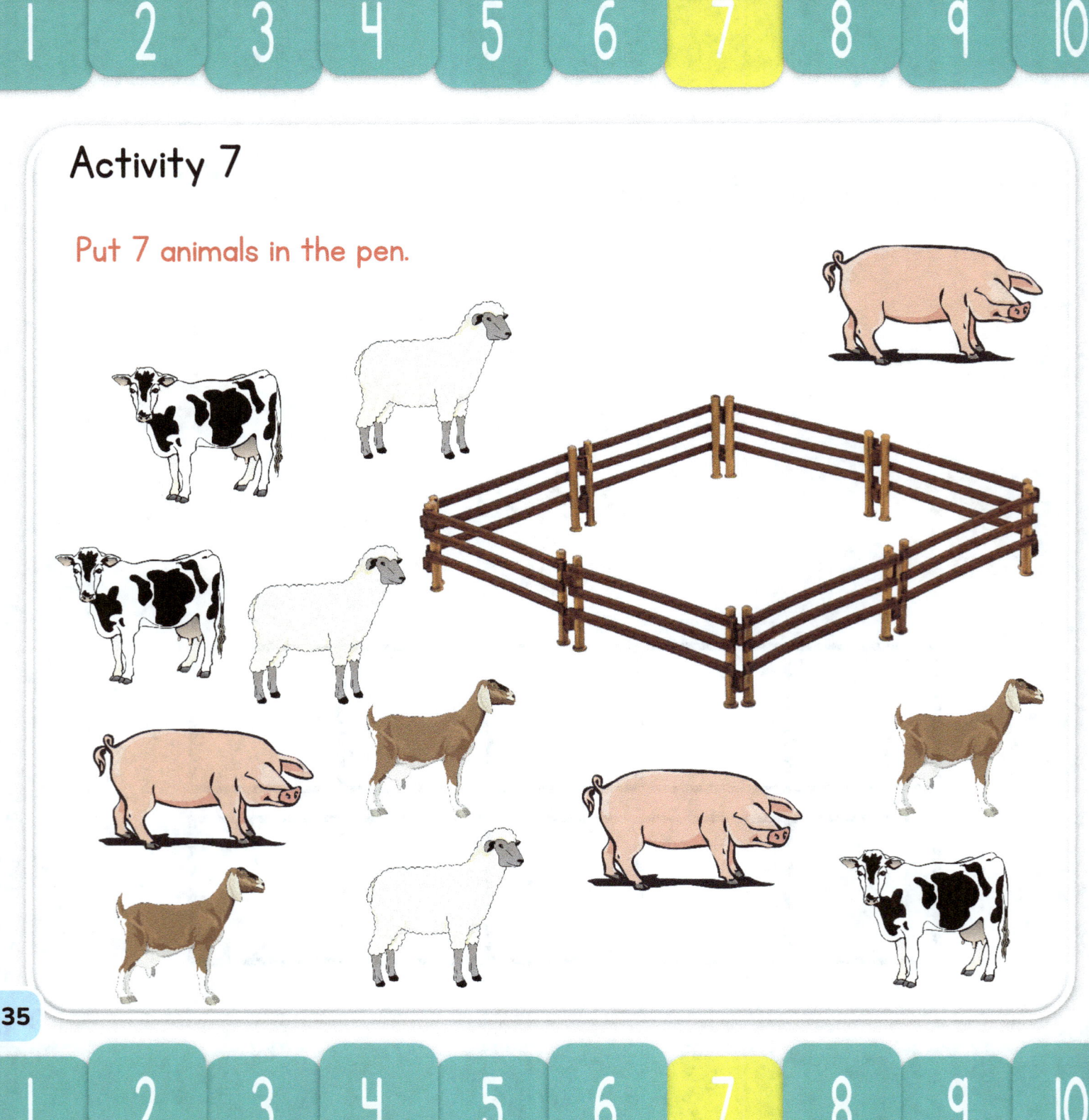

35

8 eight

Let's count 8

eight deers

eight tigers

eight lions

36

Trace number!

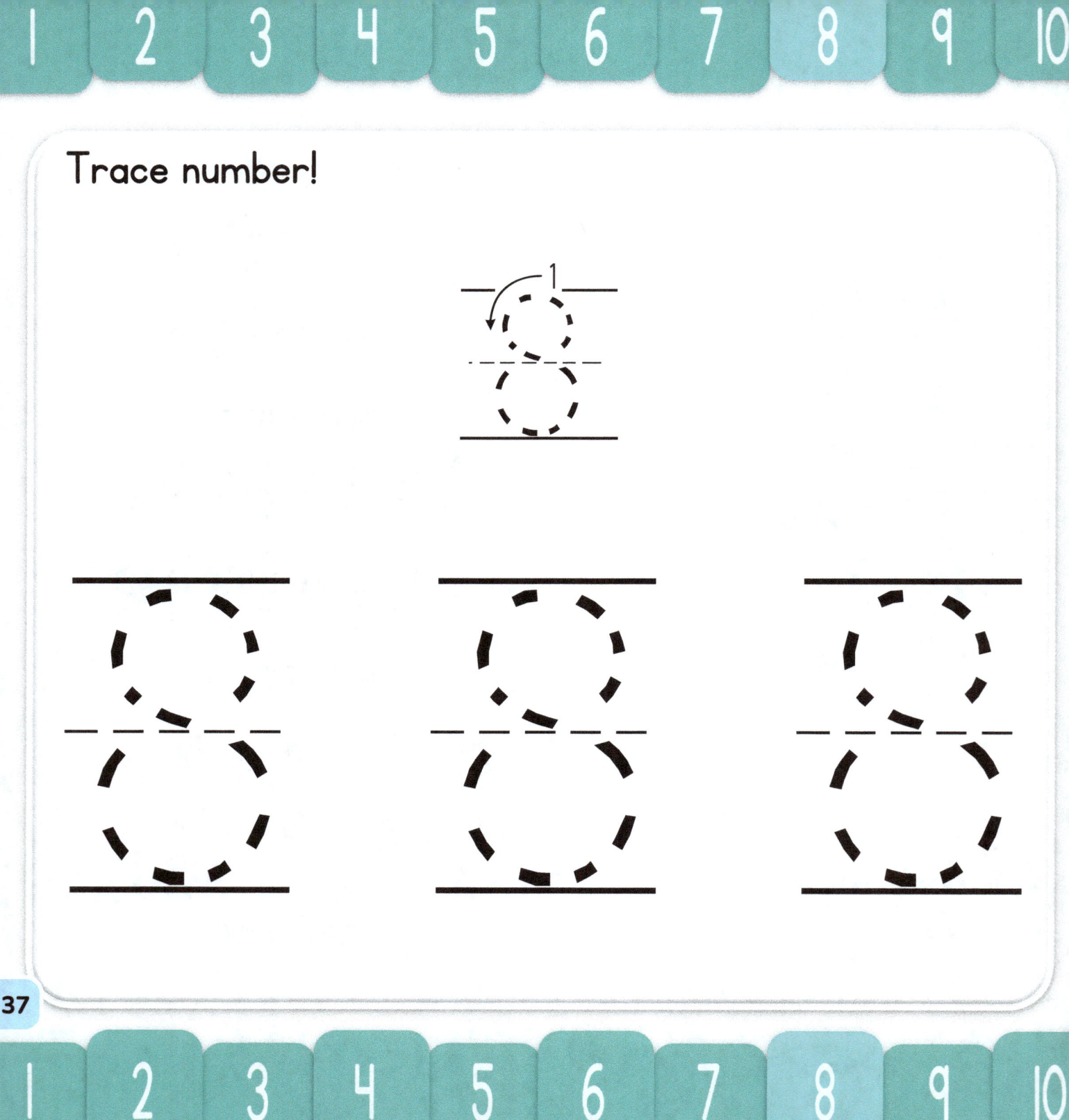

Trace number name!

eight

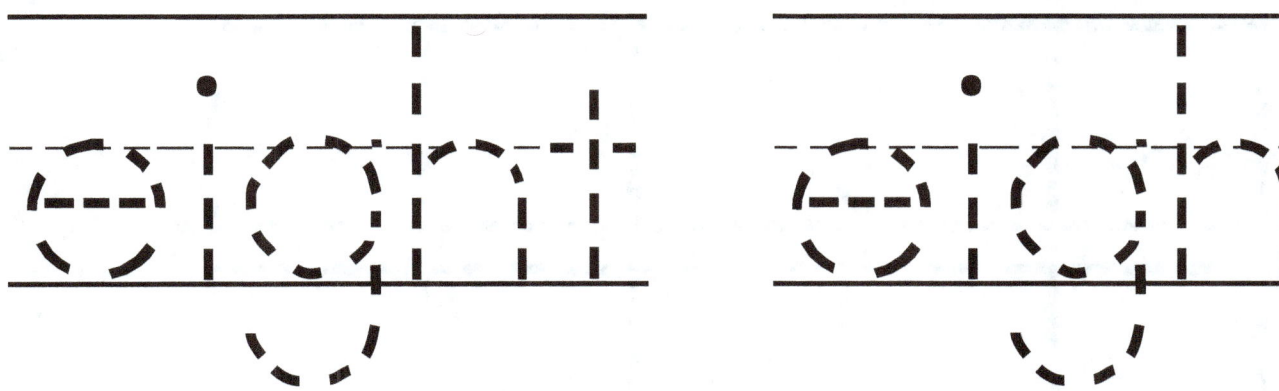

Put Counter on the frame

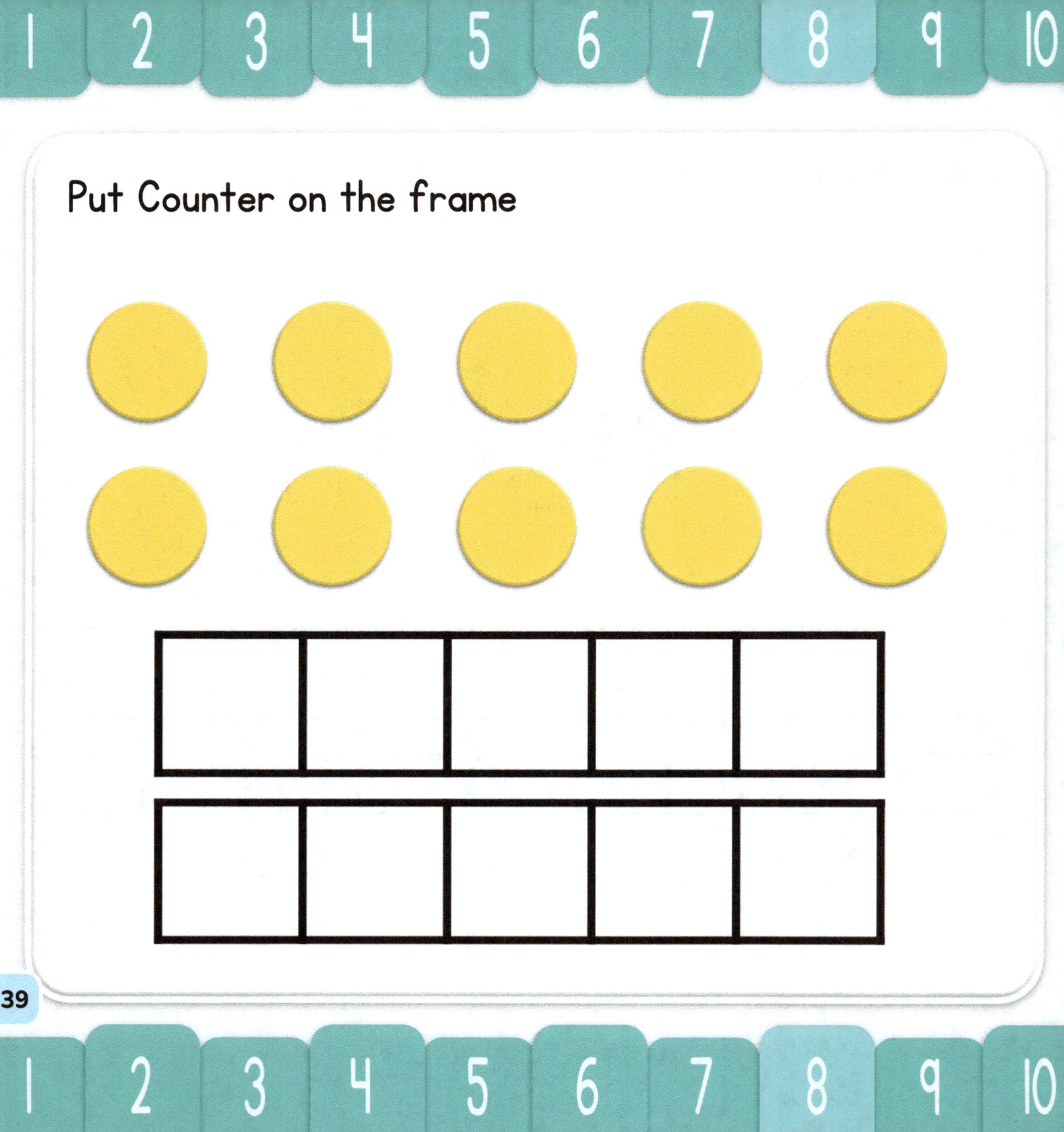

Activity 8

Cover 8 animals

q nine

Let's count 9

nine turtles

nine shrimps

nine lobsters

Trace number!

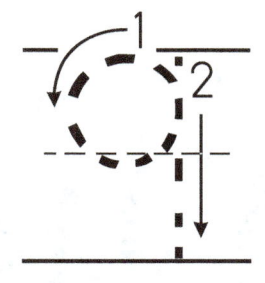

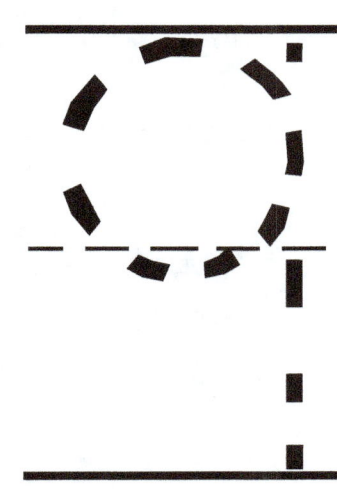
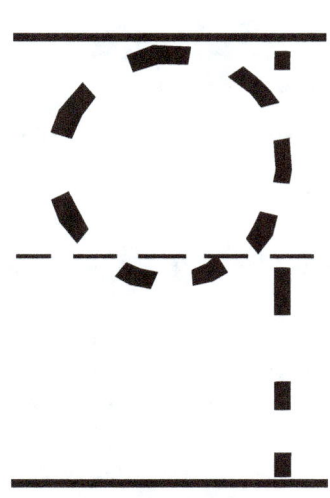
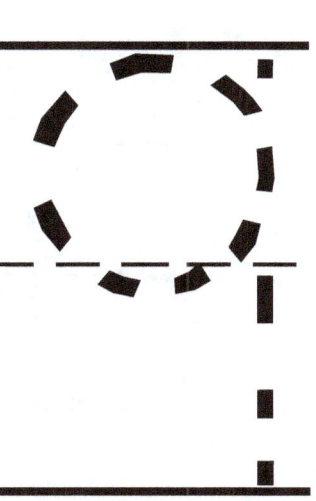

42

Trace number name!

nine

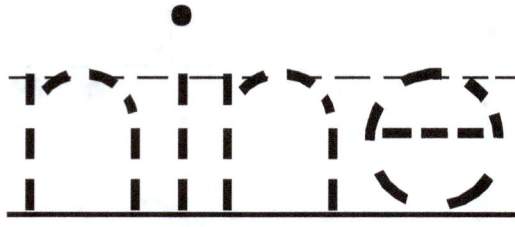 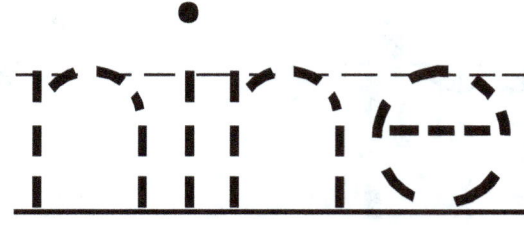

Put Counter on the frame

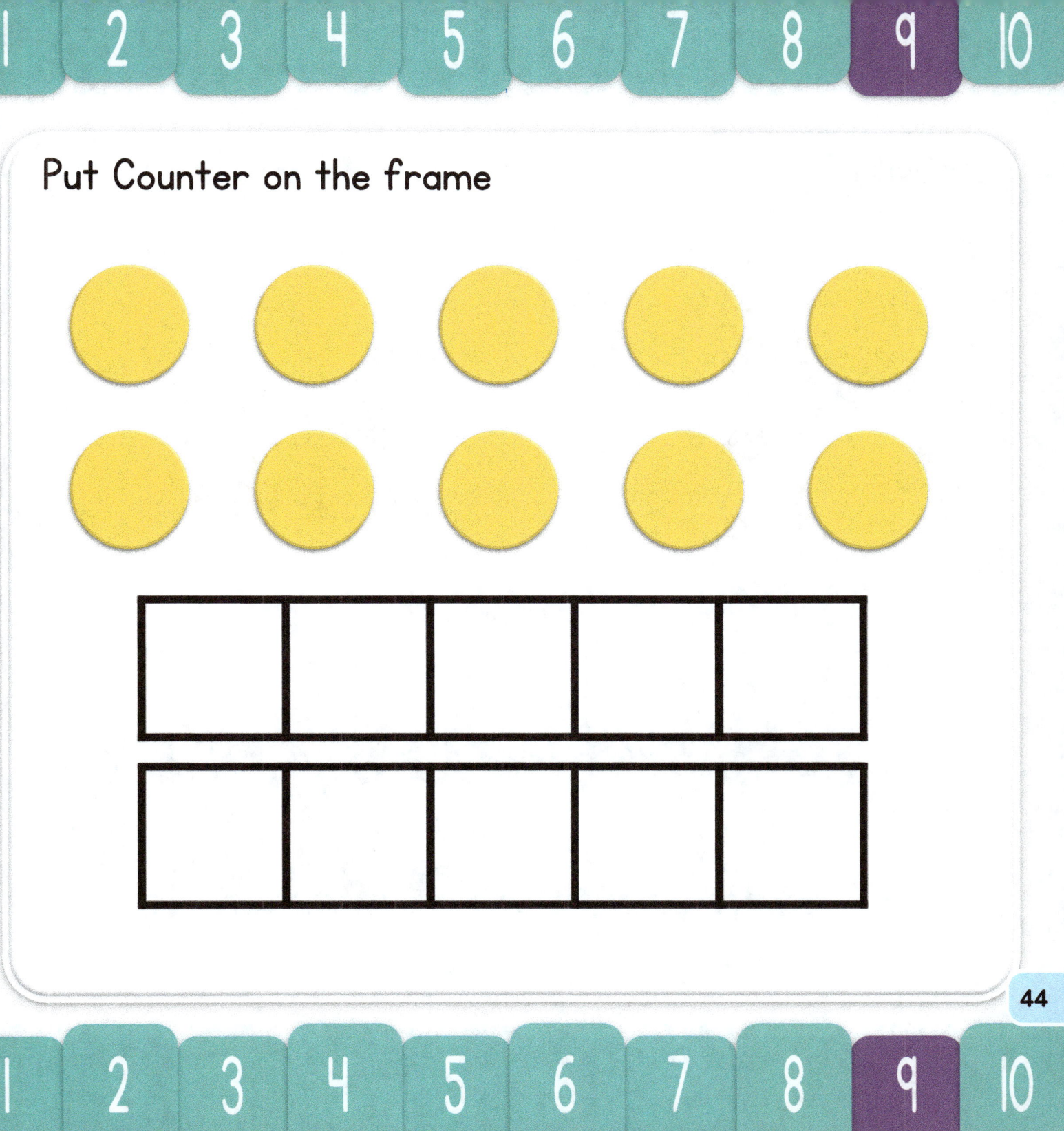

Activity 9

Choose the group with 9 shells.

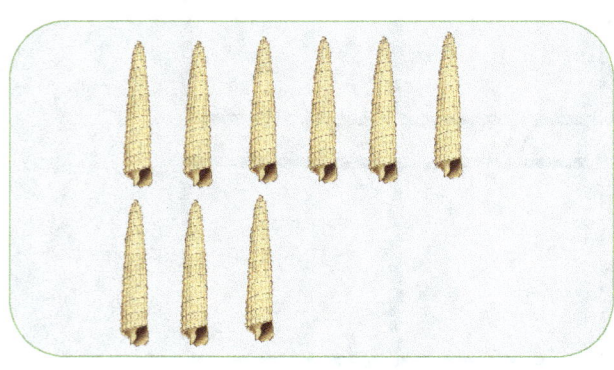

Let's count 10

ten trees

ten gifts

ten ornaments

10 ten

Trace number!

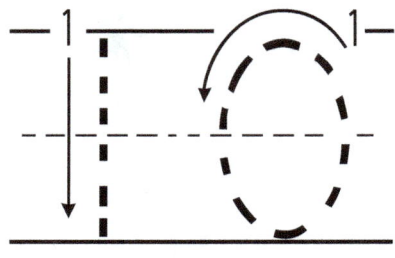

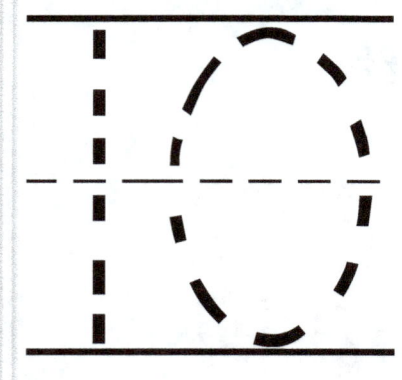

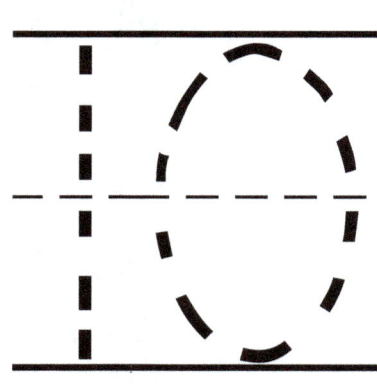

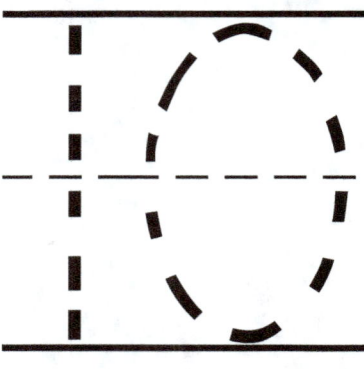

Trace number name!

ten

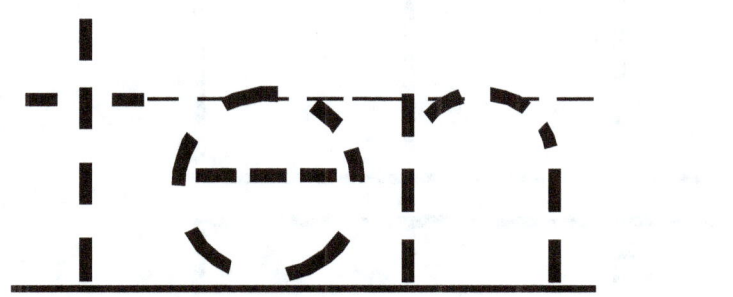 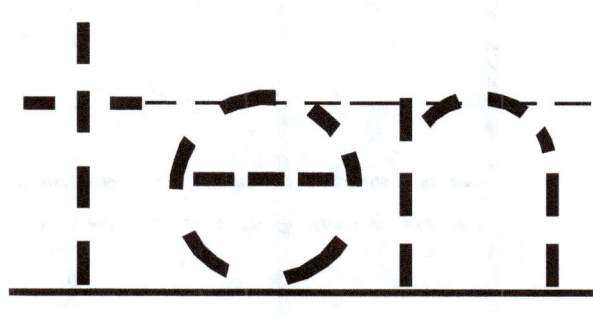

48

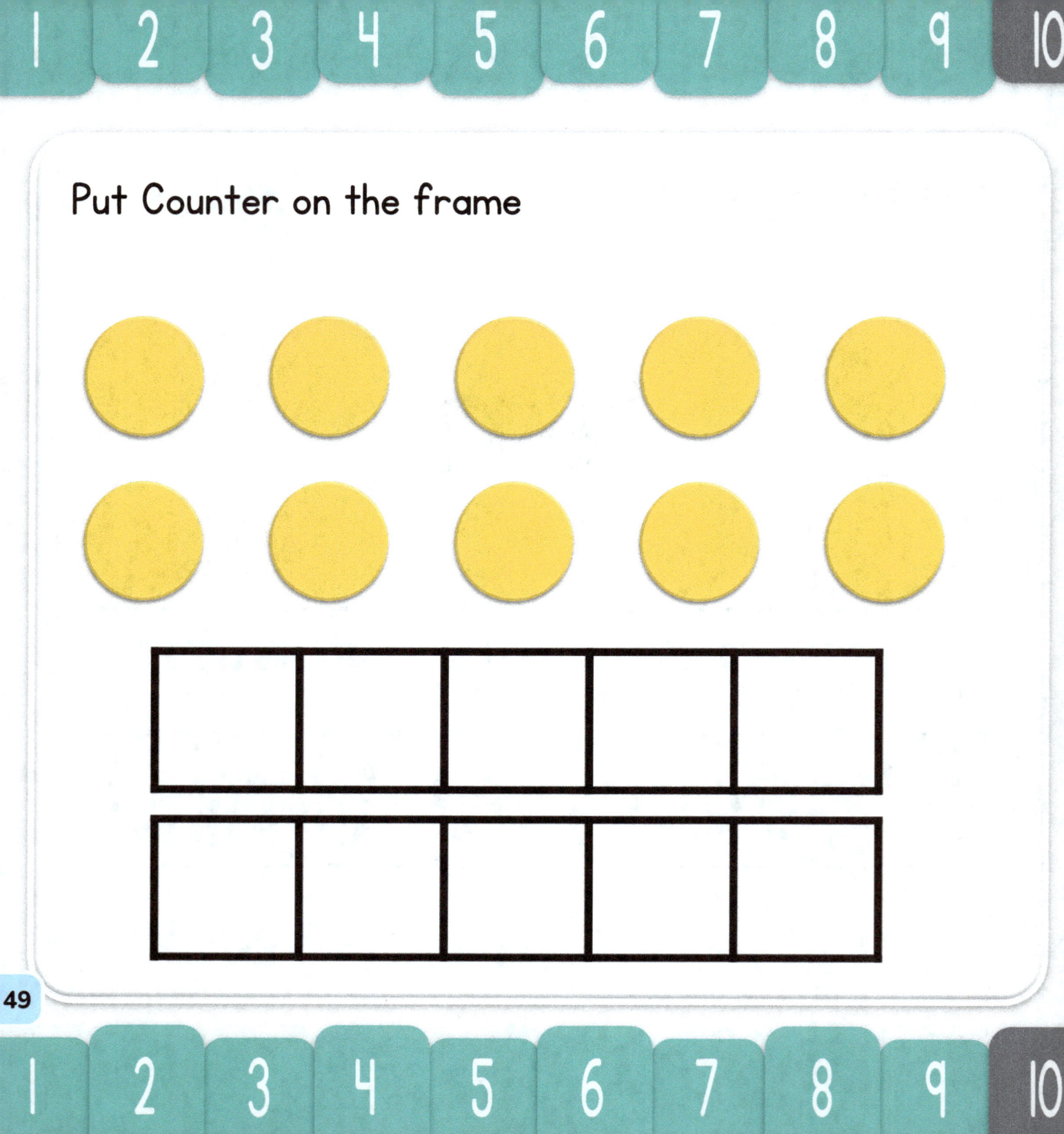

Put Counter on the frame

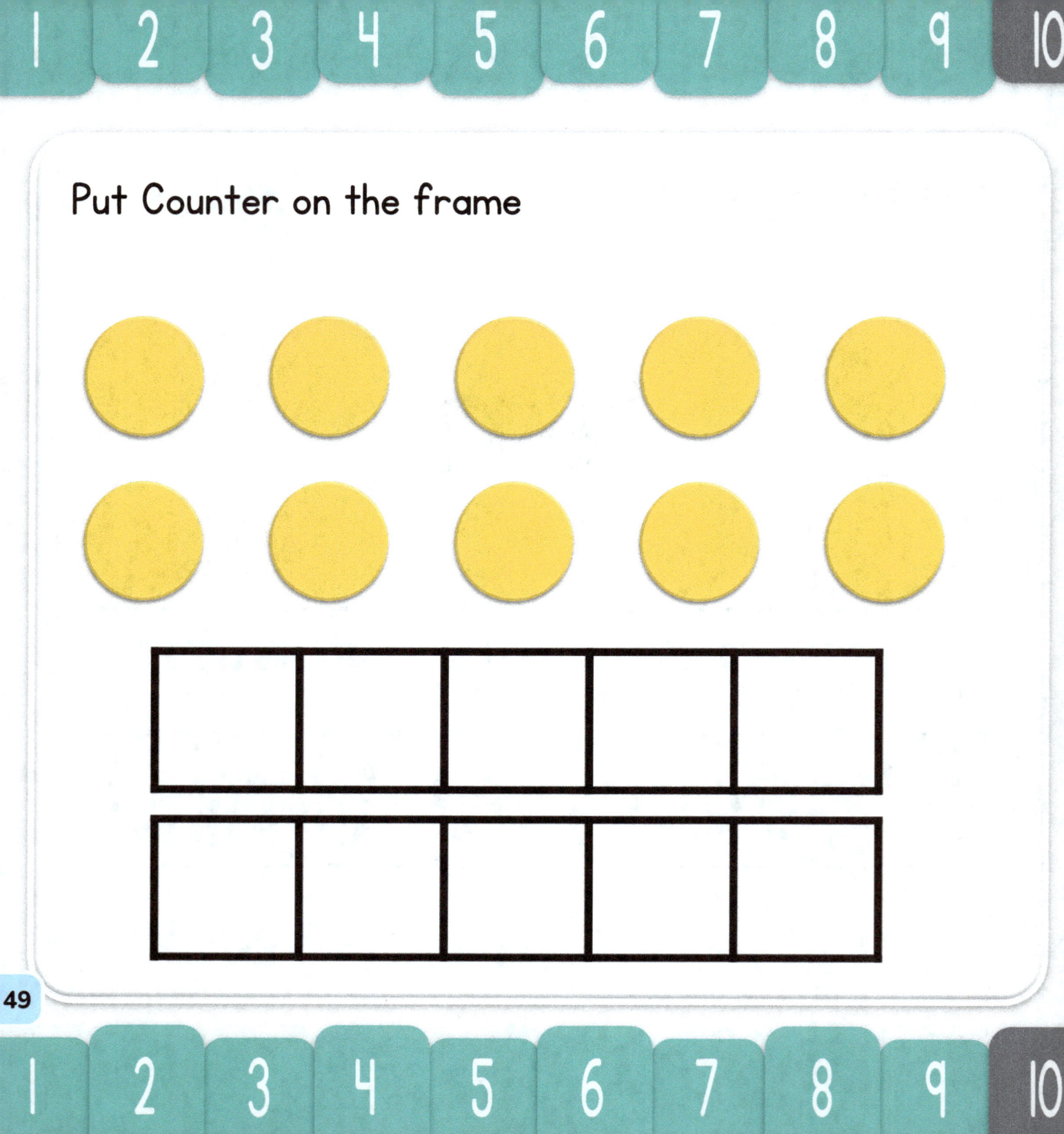

49

Activity 10

put 10 toys under the Christmas tree.